IMPERIAL PALACE

紫禁城出版社

FORBIDDEN CITY PUBLISHING HOUSE

攝　影: 宗同昌　胡　錘　林　京　許以林
　　　　　張曉巍　狄源滄　呂　劍　李毅華
　　　　　江　英　王淑琴　鄭志標
撰　稿: 劉北汜　蔡治淮
翻　譯: 李曉杰
責　編: 鄭志標

故宮

紫禁城出版社 編
紫禁城出版社出版
（北京景山前街故宮博物院內）
北京市美通印刷廠印刷
新華書店北京發行所發行
開本 787 × 1092　1/16　印張 4
1999 年 2 月第二版第二次印刷　印數 10001–30000
ISBN7-80047-087-3/J · 43
定價: 20.00 元

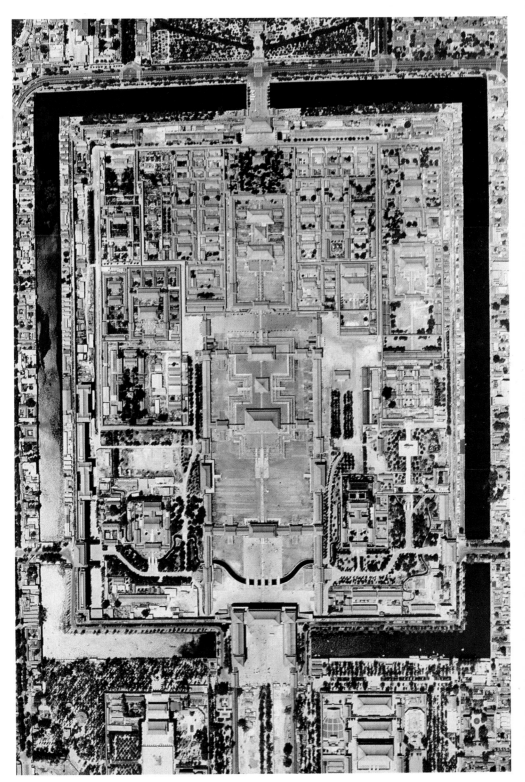

紫禁城鳥瞰 A bird's-eye view of the Forbidden City

　　故宮，即明清兩代的皇宮紫禁城，建成於永樂十八年(1420)年。
建築規模之巨，舉世無雙。明清兩代先後有二十四個皇帝住在這裡。

Construction of the Imperial Palace of the Ming and Qing Dynasties,
popularly known as the Forbidden City, started in 1406-1420(4th-18th years
of the Ming Emperor Yongle's reign). Later, it was reconstructed or restored.
It has a history of over 500 years.

1

午門

午門一角 Part of Wumen Gate

午門後背 Back of Wumen Gate

　　午門是紫禁城的正門，是朝廷頒發新的曆書，凱旋回朝的將領向皇帝進獻戰俘的重要場所。

Wumen Gate is the front entrance to the Forbidden City. During the Qing Dynasty, the ceremonies of issuing every year the lunar calendar and accepting the prisoners of war were also held here.

午門遠眺 Distant view of Wumen Gate

午門一角 Part of Wumen Gate

太和門

蜿蜒的內金水河
The meandering
Inner Golden River

太和門 Taihemen Gate

　　太和門明初稱奉天門，後稱皇極門，清初改稱太和門。明朝規定，文武官員每天拂曉到此早朝，皇帝也親來受朝和處理政務。這種活動叫做御門聽政。清初，皇帝曾在太和門受朝、賜宴等。而御門聽政在乾清門。

TAI HE MEN

晨雾中的金水桥
Bridge over the Inner
Golden River in the morning

Taihemen Gate was named Fengtianmen Gate in the early Ming Dynasty, then it was named Huangjimen Gate. The present name was given in the early Qing Dynasty. During the Ming Dynasty this gate was the place where the emperors received greetings from their high officials and dealt with state every day affairs. The Qing emperors moved to Qianqingmen Gate to listen to minister's reports and make decisions (known as "Yu Men Ting Zheng").

太和門天頂 Ceiling of Taihemen Gate

太和門前銅獅

Bronze lion in front of
Taihemen Gate

太和門前石廟

Stone temple in front of
Taihemen Gate

太和門前石印盒

Stone seal box in front of
Taihemen Gate

太和殿

太和殿匾額
Horizontal inscribed
board on Taihedian Hall

太和殿 Taihedian Hall

　　太和殿（俗稱金鑾殿），明初稱奉天殿，後稱皇極殿，清代改稱太和殿。太和殿是紫禁城中最高、最大的建築物，是明清兩代皇帝舉行盛大典禮的最主要的場所，主要包括元旦、冬至、萬壽節（皇帝的生日）、皇帝即位、皇帝大婚、冊封皇后、命將出征等重要活動。

TAI HE DIAN

Taihedian Hall, popularly called ''Jin Luan Dian'', was in the early Ming Dynasty first named Fengtiandian Hall, then named Huangjidian Hall. The present name was given in the early Qing Dynasty. The hall is 35m. high and covers an area of 2,377sq.m. It is the tallest and largest of the palace buildings. Here the Ming and Qing emperors held important ceremonies on occasions of accession, birthday, Lunar New Year, or winter solstice.

太和殿

銅爐 Bronze censers

鎏金銅缸 Gilt bronze vat

In front of Taihedian Hall can be found sundials, standard measures, bronze censers, bronze tortoises and cranes, symbolizing the longevity of the emperor and his everlasting power. For grand ceremonies incense would burn in the censers, tortoises and cranes. The spiraling smoke created a solemn and mysterious atmosphere.

嘉量 Standard Measure

日晷 Sundial

銅鶴 Bronze crane

　　太和殿前的丹墀上，陳設日晷、嘉量、銅鼎、銅龜、銅鶴，象徵
江山萬代永固，皇帝萬壽無疆。每逢大典，爐、龜、鶴內都要點燃香
料，烟霧繚繞，用來增添肅穆神秘的氣氛。

三臺上的漢白玉欄桿 White marble balustrades

铜龟 Bronze tortoise

太和殿內景 Interior view of Taihedian Hall

　　太和殿內氣派非凡，金光燦爛。正中高臺上設金漆蟠龍寶座及金漆雕龍圖屏，兩旁有六根瀝粉貼金蟠龍金柱。正對寶座上方，有一顆銀白色的大圓珠，從藻井的金漆蟠龍口裡垂下。

The magnificent interior of Taihedian Hall. On a platform in the exact centre of the hall stands a gold lacquer throne carved with coiling dragons, backed by a gold lacquer dragon screen, and flanked by six pillars entwined with coiling golden dragons. Directly above the throne a huge silver pearl hangs from the mouth of another coiling gold lacquer dragon.

金漆蟠龍寶座與金漆雕龍圍屏 The gold lacquer throne with coiling dragons, backed by a gold lacquer screen carved with dragons

太和殿內藻井
Caisson ceiling of Taihedian Hall

太和殿內景
Interior view of Taihedian Hall

中和殿内景 Interior view of Zhonghedian Hall

三臺 The three-tiered, I shaped, terraces and their white marble balustrades

中和殿 Zhonghedian Hall

中和殿是在太和殿舉行大典時，皇帝先到這裡稍事休息的地方。

Zhonghedian Hall was the place where the emperor first came to have a rest before holding ceremonies in Taihedian Hall.

保和殿後的雲龍大石雕

Carved stone pavement with **dragons and clouds** decoration at the back of Baohedian Hall

　　保和殿後的雲龍石雕是宮內石雕中最大的。石雕長 16.75 米，寬 3.07米，厚1.07米，明代雕造，清乾隆二十六年重雕。

The stone pavement with dragons and clouds decoration at the back of Baohedian Hall is 16.57m. long, 3.07m. wide and 1.70m. thick. It is the largest to have been carved during the Ming Dynasty and it was recarved in 1761, the twenty-sixth year of Qing Emperor Qianlong's reign.

保和殿 Baohedian Hall

保和殿内景 Interior view of Baohedian Hall

保和殿在明代稱謹身殿，清稱保和殿。清朝常在此舉行宴會及科舉殿試。

During the Ming Dynasty Baohedian Hall was named Jinshendian Hall. The present name was given in the early Qing Dynasty. Here banquets and final imperial examinations were held during the Qing Dynasty.

乾淸門　Qianqingmen Gate

乾淸門廣場上的鎏金銅缸
Gilt bronze vat on the square in front of Qianqingmen Gate

乾清門前鎏金銅獅 Gilt bronze lion in front of Qianqingmen Gate

乾清宮 Qianqinggong Palace

乾清宮前鎏金銅香爐 Gilt bronze incense burner in front of Qianqinggong Palace

乾清宮是明代和清初皇帝的寢宮及處理日常政務的地方。清代從雍正帝移居養心殿後，祇在這裡接見朝廷官吏、舉行宮廷宴會。

Qianqinggong Palace was the place where the emperors lived and handled routine affairs from the Ming to the Qing Dynasty. The Qing Emperor Yongzheng moved to Yangxindian Hall but still gave audience to officials of different ranks and held ceremonies of inner court or gave banquets here.

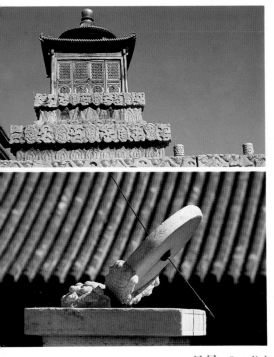

乾清宮前江山社稷方亭
The Pavilion of State Integrity
in front of Qianqinggong Palace

日晷　Sundial

乾清宮内景 Interior view of Qianginggong Palace

乾清宮内寶座 The imperial throne in Qianqinggong Palace

乾清宫内藻井 Caisson ceiling in Qianqinggong Palace

交泰殿

交泰殿內寶座
The throne in
Jiaotaidian Hall

交泰殿外景
Exterior view of
Jiaotaidian Hall

交泰殿內藻井
Caisson ceiling in
Jiaotaidian Hall

交泰殿寶座右側
陳設的大自鳴鐘，
清嘉慶三年
內務府造辦處製造，
至今還在轉動。

The chime clock
made in the palace
factory in 1798, was
also kept in Jiaotaidian Hall.
It still works.

交泰殿是皇后在元旦、
千秋（皇后的生日）等節日裡
接受朝賀的地方。乾隆年起
，這裡開始存放二十五顆皇
帝行使各方面權力的寶璽。

Jiaotaidian Hall was the place
where the empress of the
Qing Dynasty would come to
receive congratulations on her
birthday celebration and on
New Year's day. Since the
Qing Emperor Qianlong's
reign, it has been used for
storing the twenty-five
imperial seals.

交泰殿內的銅壺滴漏

The copper clepsydra in
Jiaotaidian Hall

27

坤寧宮

坤寧宮内清帝大婚洞房　Vermilion screen with golden "double-happiness" characters in the east gallery of Kunninggong Palace

坤寧宮内薩滿教祭祀場所，這裡是殺豬煮肉的神竈
The kitchen range in Kunninggong Palace for cooking
pork to be offered to the God of Manchu Lamaism

KUN NING GONG

坤寧宮清帝大婚洞房南沿大炕 The gorgeous bed in the nuptial chamber

洞房喜牀上的百子帳
The coloured curtains of the
nuptial bed with the design
of a hundred children playing

坤寧宮內清帝大婚洞房
The nuptial chamber in Kunninggong Palace

　　坤寧宮在明朝是皇后居住的正宮。清代在這裡祭神，另以東暖閣做皇帝大婚時的洞房。婚後帝及后祇在這裡住幾天，即遷居他宮。

Kunninggong Palace enclosed the bedchamber of empresses in the Ming Dynasty. During the Qing Dynasty this room was changed into a place for offering sacrifices to gods. The eastern side-room was the emperor's nuptial chamber. Only on the occasion of an imperial wedding did the royal couple stay here for several days.

御花園

堆秀山 The Mountain of Accumulated Refinement

坤寧門匾額 Horizontal inscribed
board on Kunningmen Gate

萬春亭 Wanchun Pavilion

欽安殿
Qinandian Hall

天一門 Tianyimen Gate

御花園一角 A corner of the Imperial Garden

御花園建於明代永樂十
五年，是自具一格的宮廷花
園，被譽爲宮內諸園之首。
園中的欽安殿，是故宮現存
最完整的明代建築。

御花園一角

Parts of the Imperial Garden

The Imperial Garden was built during the Ming Dynasty (15th year of Ming Emperor Yongle's reign). It has a unique style. Qinandian Hall in the garden is the most intact Ming building in the Palace Museum.

養心殿

養心殿正間寶座 The Imperial throne in the main room of Yangxindian Hall

養心殿後皇帝寢宮
The emperor's bedroom

　　養心殿建於明朝，清雍正年間重修。自雍正帝以後，清帝多在這裡居住，有好幾個皇帝死在這裡。慈禧太后曾在這裡垂簾聽政。清帝宣統退位的詔書也是在這裡簽署的。

Yangxindian Hall was built during the Ming Dynasty and restored under Qing Emperor Yongzheng's reign. From Yongzheng's reign to the end of the Qing Dynasty most of the Qing emperors lived here. A number of them died here. It was also here that Empress Dowager Cixi ruled the country from behind a screen and that Qing Emperor Xuantong signed the imperial edict of abdication after the 1911 Revolution.

養心殿鳥瞰 A bird's-eye view of Yangxindian Hall

養心門 Yangxinmen Gate

養心殿

三希堂 Room of the Three Rarities

皇帝龍牀 Emperor's bed

養心殿後皇帝寢宮
The emperor's bedroom

養心殿東暖閣兩重寶座——慈禧垂簾聽政處
Throne in the heated east room of Yangxindian Hall

西六宮

儲秀宮 Chuxiugong Palace

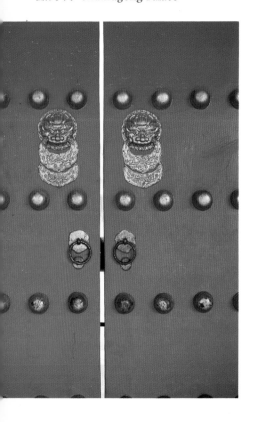

　　西六宮與東六宮的建築左右對稱，格局基本相同，都是一座座正方形的院落，院門居中，各有前後兩座殿宇及兩廂配殿，組合成兩進三合院。目前西六宮室內尚保持后妃居住時的原狀。

SIX WESTERN PALACES

西六宮鳥瞰 A bird's-eye view of the six western palaces

西二長街 Two long alleys lead to the six western palaces

儒秀宮內景 Interior view of Chuxiugong Palace

儲秀宮內一角 Interior view of Chuxiugong Palace

翊坤門 Yikunmen Gate

長春宮 Changchungong Palace

長春宮院內戲臺 The stage in the courtyard of Changchungong Palace

長春宮內陳設 Furniture in Changchungong Palace

益壽齋匾額 Horizontal inscribed board on Yishou Lodge

太極殿内陳設 Furniture in Taijidian Hall

The six eastern palaces and the six western palaces are symmetrical. Square in shape, each palace unit is a compound with the door in the middle of the front wall. The compound is divided into two courtyards, each containing one main hall and two wings. All the furniture of the six western palaces has remained just as it was when the empresses and imperial concubines of the Ming and Qing dynasties lived there.

雨花閣 The Pavilion of the Rain of Flowers

　　建於清乾隆年間的雨花閣，位於慈寧宮北春華門內，是宮中喇嘛教建築。三層樓閣，鎏金銅瓦，造型別致。

Build during Qing Emperor Qianlong's reign, the Pavilion of the Rain of Flowers is situated inside Chunhuamen Gate, north of Cininggong Palace. This pavilion, a three-storied building with gilt bronze tiles, is unique in lamaistic architecture.

建福宮東次間匾額 Horizontal inscribed board in the easter room of Jianfugong Palace

建福宮門飾 Decorated gate in Jianfugong Palace

慈寧門 Ciningmen Gate

壽康宮匾額 Horizontal inscribed board in Shoukanggong Palace

　　過世皇帝的遺孀，即太后太妃們，大多居住在慈寧宮、壽安宮、壽康宮等宮殿。這裡的佛堂也最多。

Most of the Buddhist temples were located in Cininggong Palace, Shouangong Palace and Shoukanggong Palace, the quarters of the empresses dowager and dowager secondary-consorts.

英華殿院內的菩提樹
Pipal tree in the garden of Yinghuadian Hall

東六宮、箭亭

東六宮 Six eastern palaces

箭亭 The Archery Pavilion

斷虹橋 Rainbow – cutting Bridge

橋北十八槐 The eighteen Chinese scholar-trees in the north of the bridge

外東路

九龍壁 The Nine-Dragon Wall

九龍壁局部
Part of the Nine-Dragon Wall

　　寧壽宮位於紫禁城內東北隅，今繪畫館、珍寶館所在地。原是明代仁壽宮等地，爲后妃養老之所。清康熙年間改稱寧壽宮，爲清朝太后住處。乾隆三十六年至四十一年改建，共耗銀一百四十三萬餘兩，目的是供乾隆帝執政六十年歸政後做太上皇時享用。

寧壽宮西夾道 The long western alley leading to Ningshougong Palace

寧壽宮

寧壽門 Ningshoumen Gate

寧壽門前鎏金銅獅
54 Gilt bronze lion in front of Ningshoumen Gate

Located in the northeastern corner of the Forbidden City is Ningshougong Palace, where the House of Paintings and the Treasure Houses can be found today. Originally called Renshougong Palace and used as residence for older imperial concubines during the Ming Dynasty, this group of buildings was renamed Ningshougong Palace under Qing Emperor Kangxi's reign and changed into living quarters for the Empress Dowager. Between 1771 and 1776 (thirty-sixth to forty-first years of Qing Emperor Qianlong's reign), Emperor Qianlong spent more than 1,430,000 silver taels to rebuild the palace for his own use after having abdicated in favour of his son after ruling for sixty years.

寧壽門匾額
Horizontal inscribed board on Ningshoumen Gate

壽山（玉雕）The jade mountain of longevity

頤和軒內景 Interior view of Yihe Lodge

暢音閣外景 Exterior view of the Pavilion of Pleasant Sounds

暢音閣上層內景

Interior view of the top floor
of the pavilion of Pleasant Sounds

暢音閣外景

Exterior View of
the Pavilion of Pleasant Sounds

寧壽宮花園一角
Part of the garden in
Ningshougong Palace

寧壽宮花園一角
Part of the garden in
Ningshougong Palace

倦勤齋室內小戲臺前的寶座
The throne in front of a small stage in
Juanqin Lodge

倦勤齋正間寶座
Imperial throne in the main room of
Juanqin Lodge

寧壽宮花園內的禊賞亭與流盃渠
Cup-Floating Stream in the Pavilion of the
Ceremony of Purification in Ningshougong
Palace garden

從景山遠眺神武門 Distant view of Shenwumen Gate from Jingshan Mountain